First World War
and Army of Occupation
War Diary
France, Belgium and Germany

58 DIVISION
Divisional Troops
Royal Army Medical Corps
2/3 Home Counties Field Ambulance
22 February 1915 - 22 February 1915

WO95/2997/5

Published by

The Naval & Military Press Ltd

Unit 10 Ridgewood Industrial Park,

Uckfield, East Sussex,

TN22 5QE England

Tel: +44 (0) 1825 749494

www.naval-military-press.com

www.nmarchive.com

This diary has been reprinted in facsimile from the original. Any imperfections are inevitably reproduced and the quality may fall short of modern type and cartographic standards.

© **Crown Copyright**
Images reproduced by permission of The National Archives, London, England, 2015.

Contents

Document type	Place/Title	Date From	Date To
Heading	WO95/2997-5		
Heading	67 Division To 58 Division 2/3 Home Counties Fld Amb 1915 Sep-1916 Feb		
War Diary	Sevenoaks.	15/09/1915	30/09/1915
Miscellaneous	Statement To Accompany War Diary.	02/09/1915	02/09/1915
War Diary	Sevenoaks	01/10/1915	21/10/1915
War Diary	Tonbridge	22/10/1915	22/01/1916
War Diary	Woodbridge	22/02/1915	22/02/1915

WO 95/29975

67 DIVISION TO 58 DIVISION

2/3 HOME COUNTIES FLD AMB

1915 SEP — 1916 FEB

Army Form C. 2118.

WAR DIARY
or
INTELLIGENCE SUMMARY.
(Erase heading not required.)

Instructions regarding War Diaries and Intelligence Summaries are contained in F.S. Regs., Part II and the Staff Manual respectively. Title pages will be prepared in manuscript.

Hour, Date, Place	Summary of Events and Information	Remarks and references to Appendices
Sevenoaks. Sept. 15th. 12 noon.	Visited Ightham re billets but found Col. Smith the chief Sanitary Officer already there.	
Sevenoaks. Sept. 16	Men employed in forenoon cleaning Shenden Red Lodge and Kirkella.	
Sevenoaks. Sept. 17.	Brigade Route March Sevenoaks - White Hart Hill - Fawke Farm - Stone Street - Seal Sevenoaks Heavy draught horses supplied by A.S.C. (6) 2 Officers, 71 men and three ambulance wagons marched out at 9 a.m. This was all available men owing to A.T. inoculation etc. Lt. Cummings detailed to temporary duty with 2/5th.R.W.K.Reg Lt.Vicars the R.M.O. being ill. Q.M. & Hon.Major. Hewit left for duty with 9th.Prov.Fd.Amb. at Ramsgate.	
Sevenoaks Sept. 18.	10 a.m. left for Tunbridge Wells by order of A.D.M.S. Men employed in cleaning billets.	
Sevenoaks.Sept.19.	Twenty heavy draught horses taken over by us from A.S.C 14 heavy draught horses taken away, having been given us by mistake by 2/1 & 2/2 H.C.Fd.Amb.	
Sevenoaks.Sept.21.	Medical Board held at Kirkella 10.30 to 1 p.m.	
Sevenoaks.Sept.23.	State of special vigilance 5 p.m. Fd.Amb. Wagons packed ready by 8 p.m. rations drawn at 10 p.m.	
Sevenoaks. Sept.24.	Route march to Penshurst station. Inspected there by Gen.Young marched out at 9.30 arrived at station 11-35 via.Tonbridge Rd. - White Hart - Sevenoaks Weald - Chiddingston Causeway.	
Sevenoaks Sept.24.	Pay men 11 a.m. men cleaning barracks and kit inspection	
Sevenoaks Sept.25	Church parade at Solefields Camp.	
Sevenoaks.Sept.26.	Routine. Ambulance (motor) at Fort Pitt Chatham transferring cases to make room for convoy from abroad.	
Sevenoaks.Sept. 27.		
Sevenoaks. Sept. 28.	Complete kit inspection for the purpose of getting lists of deficiencies and inspection of unserviceable articles	
Sevenoaks.Sept. 28.	Medical Board sat from 10.3p to 1 p.m.	
Sevenoaks.Sept.28. 11 a.m.	Brigadier Gen.Coombe visited Kirkella nd made enquiries about convanescents walking in the town.These turned out to be from the V.A.D. hospitals in the vicinity.	

Army Form C. 2118.

WAR DIARY
or
INTELLIGENCE SUMMARY.
(Erase heading not required.)

Instructions regarding War Diaries and Intelligence Summaries are contained in F.S. Regs., Part II and the Staff Manual respectively. Title pages will be prepared in manuscript.

Hour, Date, Place	Summary of Events and Information	Remarks and references to Appendices
Sevenoaks. Sept. 28. 10 p.m.	No N.C.O.s or men allowed in Sevenoaks village before 5 p.m. and before 1 p.m. on Saturday or Sundays. Owing to the rain all the horses put in stables in the vicinity of Kirkella.	
Sevenoaks. Sept. 29.	Lectures to the men in Shenden and Red Lodge instead of Fd. Training owing to the rain.	
Sevenoaks. Sept. 30.	Routine.	

MacAllen Major.

O.C. 2/3rd HOME COUNTIES FIELD AMBULANCE R.A.M.C.

STATEMENT TO ACCOMPANY WAR DIARY.

The progress of work of this Unit has been satisfactory. I have been compelled more or less to discontinue the squad, company and stretcher drill for some days owing to the number of men who have been vaccinnated and thus unable to use their arms. The theoretical training has however been continued.
I have made a number of promotions and appointments - Company Quartermaster Sergeant Poole has been promoted to Sergeant Major and two of my Sergeants to Staff Sergeants. I have appointed a considerable number of Lance Corporals so that now my non commissioned ranks are practically complete. The L/Cpls. who are rapidly picking up their stretcher and squad drill will be of considerable use I hope in the training and maintaining of discipline in the Unit. Owing to my shortage of Medical Officers I am compelled to leave the drilling and instructing to a considerable extent to the non commissioned Officers but I hope to have one more Medical Officer available early in September. I receive very good reports from the Commandants of the V.A.D. hospitals concerning the men detailed for duty with the V.A.D's. SErgt.Major Poole & Sergt.Major Instructor Brine are doing exceedingly well as regards the training of the bearers and the Unit has improved considerably since their arrival. Discipline is well maintained. The Quartermasters Department is exceedingly well managed, mobilization equipment is being rapidly completed. We are still deficient in our complement of horses. The Medical Equipment is not complete, but we are practically complete in one section. The shortage of Medical

Officers is very serious, the medical officers having a great deal too much to do and as I have stated are unable to give much attention the the training of the bearers. I regret that I am unable to fill up the v vacanies more rapidly - Medical Officers preferring to join as temporary Lieutenants rather than join the Territorial Force.

[Signature] Major.

O.C. 2/3rd HOME COUNTIES FIELD AMBULANCE R.A.M.C.

Kirkella.
Sevenoaks.
2-9-15.

Army Form C. 2118.

WAR DIARY
or
INTELLIGENCE SUMMARY.
(Erase heading not required.)

2/3 (NC) Field Amb.

Instructions regarding War Diaries and Intelligence Summaries are contained in F.S. Regs., Part II. and the Staff Manual respectively. Title pages will be prepared in manuscript.

Hour, Date, Place	Summary of Events and Information	Remarks and references to Appendices
8.30 a.m. 1-10-15 Sevenoaks	Brigade Route march – White Hart – Ide Hill, Westerham, Brasted, Riverhead – Sevenoaks. Pte Hoghen fell out and has been admitted to hospital.	
9am to 1pm 2/10/15 "	Cleaning barracks & arranging kit	
10 am 3/10/15 "	Church Parade at Solefields Camp, afterwards voluntary service held here for each	
4/10/15 "	C.O. returned from north and leave 12.58 p.m. Routine examination held for 5th Rate of Corps Pay. Most of the candidates qualifies in written & oral exam.	
10.15 a.m. 5/10/15 "	Brigade paraded at Vine St. Cricket Ground to find munition workers. Eleven of the Unit sent in names.	
10.30 am 5/10/15 "	Medical Board met at Kit Ella.	
6/10/15 "	Regimental stretcher bearers at drill & instruction with S.A. troops. Made a number of promotions & appointments published in daily orders.	
7/10/15 "	Unloaded waggons & stored the equipment in cellars. Men employed in cleaning barracks, kit after unloading. New training in Knole Park under Capt. Matthews. Capt. Browning ill in bed. Capt. Cumings in V.A.D. Hospital and at meat board.	
8/6/15 "	Capt. Matthews at lecture Whinfield Street (G.F Order)	

Army Form C. 2118.

WAR DIARY
or
INTELLIGENCE SUMMARY.
(Erase heading not required.)

Instructions regarding War Diaries and Intelligence Summaries are contained in F.S. Regs., Part II. and the Staff Manual respectively. Title pages will be prepared in manuscript.

Hour, Date, Place	Summary of Events and Information	Remarks and references to Appendices
8/10/15 Seawards.	A.D.M.S. visited Shinchu & Kirkhilla. I went to Tunbridge Wells to see A.D.M.S. We met at Tunbridge. Conversed about billets & sanitation of Kirkhilla.	
9/10/15 "	Leave Shinchu & go to billets with two sections. Got order to leave Seaton into billets mostly about St John Chambers.	
10/10/15 "	Moved two Sections into billets mostly about St John Chambers. Searched thoroughly cleaned out. C.O. at 1 Whinpole Street - lecture - Church Parade at Solfields Camp. Special service in want for patients. C.O. 24 hours leave at Snettisham to meet Lt. Col.	
11/10/15 "	Could see funeral business of 3rd H.C. 7th Ambs. Men still in new billets and ration parties arranged. Training as usual. Capt. Browning at lecture 1 Whinpole Street.	
12/10/15 "	Went shots. Capt. Browning at lecture 1 Whinpole Street.	
13/10/15 "	Medical Board at Kirkhilla which had to be adjourned owing to failure to attend of several men who were warned. Adjourned Medical Board met. Men shaking blankets at 6 a.m. Owing to rain all men at Red Lodge, Kit- Inspection & lecture. Regimental Stretcher Bearers here at lecture.	
14/10/15 "	Men billets inspected. Corps work routine.	
15/10/15 "	Capt. Browning ill in bed. 1 week's leave granted.	
16/10/15 "		
16/10/15 "	Morning wash drill & lecture, afternoon pay of Units & physical drill	
17/10/15 "	Men employed Kit-Inspection cleaning barrack rooms etc. Solfields Camp Special service in hospital	

Army Form C. 2118.

WAR DIARY
or
INTELLIGENCE SUMMARY.
(Erase heading not required.)

3.

Hour, Date, Place	Summary of Events and Information	Remarks and references to Appendices
9 a.m. 18 Oct. Sevenoaks	C.O. with Lt. Eyre & S. Major at Tonbridge seeing to billets for Unit & hospital premises.	
19" "	Capt. Matthews, S. Major + a party at Tonbridge having billets allotted to men. They report billets available not sufficient, London Rd being our area with no side roads, practically to accommodation. Pushing wagon.	
20th "	Capt. Matthews again in Tonbridge on the Quartering Committee. will not give us an empty house. He has arranged that the transport sleep in a barn over the stable.	
8.45 21" "	Parade moved off at 9.30 had to wait at High Street, and of Oak have for regiment to pass. Made our point up to turn with the assistance of the bearers and sent Dioramas who had to push the wagons up every hill owing to the fact that we have no heavy draught horses. Arrived at new station at 1 p.m. Got the men to their billets &	
9 a.m. 22 " Tonbridge	had rations served at 3 o'clock. We have spent a night Parade in field opposite hospital.	
23rd "	20 beds, last night had six available. got 9 no faint in on hospital. Capt. Matthews who was left with the rear party returned. 48 hours leave to London	

C.O.
Forms/C. 2118/10.

Army Form C. 2118.

WAR DIARY
or
INTELLIGENCE SUMMARY.
(Erase heading not required.)

4.

Hour, Date, Place	Summary of Events and Information	Remarks and references to Appendices
24 Oct. Tonbridge	Church Parade at Parish Church.	
25 " "	A.D.M.S. visited hospital. Men employed routine.	
26 " "	Routine, physical drill & lecture drill	
27 " "	Routine. Capt. Cunning delivered a lecture on Venereal Disease, prevention, cure & precautions.	
28 " " "	Visited V.A.D. Hospital Quarry Hill. Men marched out after dinner. Lecture & preparation for examination in first aid tomorrow.	
29 " " "	Capt. Matthews & Cunning conducting exam. in 1st aid. Borrowed motor ambulance to remove case of pneumonia to V.A.D.	
30 " "	Men employed kit inspection & cleaning barracks.	
31 " "	Church Parade.	

Markham Lt. Col.
O.C. 2/3rd Home Counties
Field Ambulance R.A.M.C.

Army Form C. 2118.

WAR DIARY
or
INTELLIGENCE SUMMARY.
(Erase heading not required.)

2/3 (H.C.) Field Amb.

Hour, Date, Place	Summary of Events and Information	Remarks and references to Appendices
Cambridge 1/11/15	Do. Very wet. Men employed in morning lectures & practical work. In afternoon 62 men sent to billets to Found for tomorrows examination. Capt. Cummings taking over Headquarters & Cottage	M
2/11/15	The examination for the men who have applied for Corps Pay concluded today. 28 qualified out of 62. Inspected Madan House re taking it over for billets. Men employed as usual, drills, physical drills. Except those for examination. Weather fine but cold.	M
3/11/15	A.D.M.S. 2nd. Division visited Reception Hospital & inspected proposed house for observation hospital. Men employed. Route march. Stretcher drill. lecture in afternoon. I inspected transport and transport billets and found everything greatly improved.	M
4/11/15	A.D.M.S. 2nd. Army visited the Brigade Area. made various suggestions about the billets and came to the Reception Hospital about noon. He expressed his pleasure generally about the hospital and gave directions about a new bath.	M
5/11/15	Men employed in drills in morning lectures and physical drill in afternoon.	M
6/11/15	Col.Smith Divl.S.O. arrived here to inspect billets re the report of Col.Slossonn. Pay of men in morning drills and lectures. Afternoon physical drill. The medical board on Lieut.Thomas R.E. held in afternoon and forwarded to A.D. M.S. by cyclist.	M
	Officers moving into cottage. Medical Inspection of troops. Kit inspection. Visited Bde. Office re baths for Brigade.	M
7/11/15	Church parade at Parish Church. 2 in hospital. Board on Capt. Powdrigg. Rowbriggs at Surbiton. President. Lt.Col.Berkley, members. Capt. Mathews & Lt. Hamilton.	M

Army Form C. 2118.

WAR DIARY
or
INTELLIGENCE SUMMARY.
(Erase heading not required.)

Instructions regarding War Diaries and Intelligence Summaries are contained in F.S. Regs., Part II. and the Staff Manual respectively. Title pages will be prepared in manuscript.

Hour, Date, Place	Summary of Events and Information	Remarks and references to Appendices
Tonbridge. 8/11/15.	Drills before noon and practical work. Afternoon lectures. Board of Enquiry held on Winkle of 2/5th.R.W.Kent.Regt. adjourned. Medical Board met at 10.30. Resumed Board of enquiry met again at Reception Hospital.	ces
13/11/15.	very wet day, men employed indoors. lectures and practical work. Visited V.A.D. in afternoon. Cpl's sent to Tunbridge Wells for clinkers and bus for the entrance. Left 10.45 a.m. arrived back 7.45 p.m. great difficulty with the mules, which fell on the setts. Capt. Matthews inspected Dryhill House reported one room unclean. Men - march in morning, drill in afternoon.	ces
1/11/15.	Found Hawdon Farm not available for observation Hospital, family having not yet left.	ces
16/11/15.	Visit by A.D.M.S. 67th.H.C.Division.	ces
22/11/15.	Aeroplane made a voluntary descent near hospital. found to be british.	ces
23/11/15.	Dense fog all day.	ces
24/11/15.	Bright clear day.	ces
25/11/15.	A.D.M.S. 2nd. ARMY and A.D.M.S. 67th.Division. visited this Reception Hospital to approve of discharge of recruits and soldiers which had been recommended by the Standing Medical Board. They also inspected the Reception Hospital.	ces

Markey Lt.Col.
2/3RD HOME COUNTIES
O.C. FIELD AMBULANCE R.A.M.C,

Army Form C. 2118.

WAR DIARY
~~INTELLIGENCE SUMMARY~~ E.m.
(Erase heading not required.)

Instructions regarding War Diaries and Intelligence Summaries are contained in F.S. Regs., Part II. and the Staff Manual respectively. Title pages will be prepared in manuscript.

213 H.C. F Coy.

Hour, Date, Place	Summary of Events and Information	Remarks and references to Appendices
Tonbridge Dec 1st	nil	
Dec 2nd 11:10 am	Visit & Inspection by Major General Young. G.O.C. 67th Division & Col Gordon. A.A. & Q.M.G. (67th Division). Appeared well satisfied with the arrangements & workings of the Hospital	E.m.
Dec 3rd	nil	
Dec 4th	Visit by A.D.M.S. 67th A.B. Division	E.m.
9-50 pm	Fire at Supply Depot of forage	E.m.
Dec 5th	nil	
Dec 6th	nil	
Dec 7th 1-50 pm	Urgent secret call for Horse Ambulance, Statcher Party & Medical Officer to proceed to 202 High Street 24 The Buffs	E.m.
	On arrival there, the party was inspected and dismissed.	
Dec 8th	nil	
Dec 9th 10-30 am	Visit by A.D.M.S. 67th A.B. Division	E.m.

Army Form C. 2118.

WAR DIARY

INTELLIGENCE SUMMARY.

(Erase heading not required.)

Instructions regarding War Diaries and Intelligence Summaries are contained in F.S. Regs., Part II. and the Staff Manual respectively. Title pages will be prepared in manuscript.

Hour, Date, Place	Summary of Events and Information	Remarks and references to Appendices
Larkhill Dec 9th 11 a.m.	No. 3. Travelling Medical Board attended here for purpose of classifying men of the 202nd Inf. Brigade, recommended by Medical Boards to discharge	
Dec 10th	nil	
Dec 11th	nil	
Dec 12th	nil	
Dec 13th	nil	
Dec 14th	nil	
Dec 15th	nil	
Dec 16th	nil	
Dec 17th	nil	
Dec 18th 12 noon	Visit by A.D.M.S. 67th (2nd.) Division	
Dec 19th	nil	
Dec 20th	nil	
Dec 21st	nil	
Dec 22nd	nil	
Dec 23rd	nil	

Army Form C. 2118.

WAR DIARY
or
INTELLIGENCE SUMMARY. ~~Erm~~

(Erase heading not required.)

Instructions regarding War Diaries and Intelligence Summaries are contained in F. S. Regs., Part II. and the Staff Manual respectively. Title pages will be prepared in manuscript.

Hour, Date, Place	Summary of Events and Information	Remarks and references to Appendices
Tonbridge Dec 24th	Visit by A.D.M.S 67th (H.C.) Division	Ewm
Dec 25th 11 a.m	Visit by Divisional Sanitary Officer (Col Smith) to Tonbridge Brigade Area re latrine accommodation & mess rooms	Ewm
Dec 26th	nil	
Dec 27th	nil	
Dec 28th	nil	
Dec 29th	nil	
Dec 30th	nil	
Dec 31st	nil	

Ewmwitsw kept in
O.C 2ND/3RD HOME COUNTIES
FIELD AMBULANCE R.A.M.C.

Army Form C. 2118.

WAR DIARY

INTELLIGENCE SUMMARY.

(Erase heading not required.)

Instructions regarding War Diaries and Intelligence Summaries are contained in F.S. Regs., Part II. and the Staff Manual respectively. Title pages will be prepared in manuscript.

Hour, Date, Place	Summary of Events and Information	Remarks and references to Appendices
1916		
Jany 3 Tonbridge	Visit and inspection of "Sandycombe" Reception Hospital by Major General. Young. G.O.C. 64th (H.C.) Division	
" 4 "	Visit by A.D.M.S 64th (H.C.) Division	Evm.
" 6 "	Visit by A.D.M.S 64th (H.C.) Division	Evm.
" 12 " 10.a.m	Inspection of Field Ambulance and Reception Hospital by the D.D.M.S. Central Force.	Evm.
" 22 "	Visit by A.D.M.S 64th (H.C.) Division	Evm.

E W Mawson
O.C. Capt for
2ND/3RD HOME COUNTIES
FIELD AMBULANCE R.A.M.C.

Army Form C. 2118.

2/3RD HOME COUNTIES
FIELD AMBULANCE R.A.M.C.

WAR DIARY
or
INTELLIGENCE SUMMARY.
(Erase heading not required.)

Instructions regarding War Diaries and Intelligence Summaries are contained in F. S. Regs., Part II. and the Staff Manual respectively. Title pages will be prepared in manuscript.

Hour, Date, Place	Summary of Events and Information	Remarks and references to Appendices
Woolwich. 27/5/15. 3.15 pm	Arrived from Tonbridge having been transferred from the 67th N.C. Division to the 58th (London) Division. "A" section remains here, while "B" & "C" sections proceeded to Ufford where they are billeted	Encl.

78. New Street
Woolbridge
2-3-16

J. Merkley Lt. Col.
O.C. 2/3RD HOME COUNTIES
FIELD AMBULANCE R.A.M.C.

www.ingramcontent.com/pod-product-compliance
Lightning Source LLC
Chambersburg PA
CBHW081510160426
43193CB00014B/2645